Published 2021 by Kingfisher
Published in the United States by Kingfisher.
120 Broadway. New York. NY 10271
Kingfisher is an imprint of Macmillan Children's Books. London

ISBN: 978-0-7534-7638-3

Designed by: Collette Sadler
Edited by: Kath Jewitt/Elizabeth Yeates
Illustrated by: Sarah Lawrence/Advocate Art

Library of Congress Cataloguing-in-Publication data
has been applied for.

Kingfisher books are available for special promotions and
premiums. For details contact: Special Markets Department.
Macmillan. 120 Broadway. New York. NY 1027

Printed in China
9 8 7 6 5 4 3 2 1
1TR/1220/WKT/UG/128MA

Picture credits
The Publisher would like to thank the following for permission to reproduce their material.
Top = t: Bottom = b: Center = c: Left = l: Right = r
15t: Thinnapob Proongsak/Shutterstock: 15b: ssuaphotos/Shutterstock: 24: NASA: 26-27 marinat197/
Shutterstock: 27: Nicolas Primola/Shutterstock: 30cr Siwakorn1933/Shutterstock: 30b Evan Lorne/
Shutterstock: 31t Elena Larina/Shutterstock: 31c Nokuro/Shutterstock: 31b Ronedya/Shutterstock.

ECO HERO ACADEMY

TRAINING PROGRAM

THEORY

PRACTICAL

THEORY pages are full of important information that you need to know.

PRACTICAL pages have a task to do or a coding skill to acquire. Check off each page when you have completed that part of your training.

TRAINING TIME

So you want to be an Eco Hero? Do you love nature and want to protect the planet?
Do you like working outside and investigating?
Then ecology is perfect for you!

WHAT DOES AN ECOLOGIST DO?

Ecologists are scientists who think of ways plants, animals, and people can live together side by side with the environment.

They record how living things interact with each other.

Ecologists go into the field—that means working outdoors!

They study how living things share natural resources like water, air, and food.

THEORY NO. 1 APPROVED

ECO VOCAB

What is the environment?
It is everything in the world around us that is living and nonliving. Living things include plants, animals —and us! Nonliving things are water, air, and land.

What are natural resources?
These are materials that are produced by the environment. Water, oil, plants, and animals are all examples of natural resources.

They use this information to find ways to protect the world and make it a better place for everyone.

Ecologists monitor the impact that humans have on the environment.

ACTIVITY

Which of these are natural resources?

○ Water

○ Car

○ Cell Phone

○ Rubber Duck

○ Banana

7

PRACTICAL 1

ECO HERO ACADEMY

An Eco Hero needs more than a cape to save the world! Here are some of the things you will need to do . . .

PROTECT animals and plants.

CARE about the future of our planet.

STUDY science, math, geography and information technology (IT) in school.

WORK in all weather and even at night!

NOTICE big and small changes in the world.

There are many different jobs you can do if you're an ecologist. Some will take you up the highest mountains or down to the deepest ocean floors. You could find yourself working in a lab, teaching, or even writing laws to protect the environment. Which of these jobs would you most like to do?

PLAN the best route for a new road so it doesn't harm wildlife.

RUN an endangered species breeding program at a zoo.

DESIGN an ocean reserve to protect marine life.

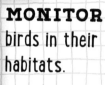

MONITOR birds in their habitats.

TEST if chemicals in a river are bad for the environment.

BUILD a computer model to monitor pollution levels.

MAKE movies, books, and TV shows about wildlife.

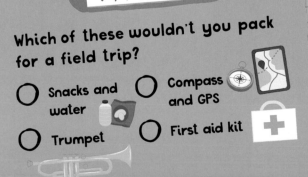

ACTIVITY

Which of these wouldn't you pack for a field trip?

○ Snacks and water

○ Compass and GPS

○ Trumpet

○ First aid kit

OUR BEAUTIFUL BIOSPHERE

Ecologists look at the world differently from most people. They divide it into six levels to explain all the ways we are all connected to each other.

THEORY NO. 2 APPROVED

Individuals that are related to each other are called a species—human beings are a species. Where an individual lives is called a habitat—your home is your habitat.

1. INDIVIDUAL
This is a single living organism. From a tiny microbe to the biggest predator, we are all individuals. That includes you!

DID YOU KNOW?
There are 1,000s of good bacteria living inside you, and they are a population!

There are ecosystems all over Earth—on land and in the water. They can be microscopic, like a drop of water, or huge, like the oceans, which cover 70% of the planet!

2. POPULATION When groups of the same individuals live in the same area.

3. COMMUNITY When many different populations live in the same ecosystem.

4. ECOSYSTEM An ecosystem is a collection of communities that live in the same area and share natural resources such as air and water.

5. BIOME A biome is a big area, like a forest or desert. Each has different weather and temperatures. with many plants and animals that can only live there.

6. BIOSPHERE All of the biomes together make up the biosphere. Planet Earth is a biosphere. We are all part of the biosphere—humans, plants, animals, and microorganisms.

ACTIVITY

Count how many species you can find next time you are at the park.

MISSION ECO HERO

Ecologists spend a lot of time in the field collecting information (data) about the health of ecosystems. Let's dive in for a close look at a very special ecosystem—a tropical coral reef.

Mangrove trees protect coral reefs by stopping soil from falling into the water and smothering the reef.

The tree roots clean the water and make healthy food for the animals that live in the reef.

Coral reefs have been around for more than 200 million years. About 25% of all ocean animals live in coral reefs!

Can you spot these animals hiding in the coral?

○ Turtle
○ Octopus
○ Clown fish
○ Crab

ACTIVITY

Boats and fishing can harm coral reefs. Ecologists have worked with governments to put many coral reefs in a sanctuary. This means fishing boats won't be allowed here.

PRACTICAL NO. 2 APPROVED

Ecologists record the creatures living in the reef. Fish keep the coral healthy by eating seaweed and the starfish that eat coral!

This ecologist is taking water samples to test in a lab. If the water gets too warm or polluted, it can kill the coral.

Coral is a tiny animal called a coral polyp that has built a hard shell around itself. The polyps join together to form a reef.

ECO ENERGY

ECO HERO MISSION

Make it your mission to turn off any lights that don't need to be switched on. Ask your friends and family to do the same.

We all use energy every day in millions of ways. Some of the things we use it for are obvious, and others aren't. We use energy to . . .

Light up buildings, rooms, and streets.

Put food on our plates.

Make everything we buy and use.

Travel.

Heat up and cool down our homes.

FOSSIL FUELS

Over millions of years, dead plants and animals turn into oil, coal, and natural gas—these are known as fossil fuels. Most of the energy we use comes from burning fossil fuels, which makes a lot of carbon dioxide and harms our planet. Fossil fuel supplies will eventually run out, so alternatives need to be used.

ECO SOLUTIONS

Scientists have developed clever ways to make energy from other resources. These are called renewable because they will never run out. Some are also called "clean" because they do not put carbon dioxide into the air.

Here are 4 types of renewable energies.

SOLAR POWER

Solar panels collect sunlight and turn it into energy such as electricity. The solar panels can be expensive to build.

GEOTHERMAL ENERGY

This is made when water is sent deep underground to be heated up by really, really hot rocks. The steam that comes off the water is turned into energy by special machines. Sometimes poisonous gases escape with the steam.

WIND POWER

Turbine blades are spun around by the wind to power up a machine that makes electricity. Turbines can only be built in windy places, and the blades can harm flying animals.

TIDAL/WAVE POWER

Turbines are also put in rivers or the ocean, where the blades are moved by the power of very fast currents and waves.

PRACTICAL
NO. 3
APPROVED

GREENHOUSE GASES

Temperatures on Earth are rising faster than ever before in human history. This rise is called global warming, and it is caused by the enhanced greenhouse effect.

GREENHOUSES

A greenhouse is a glass building where gardeners grow plants. When the Sun shines in, heat gets trapped and keeps the temperature nice and warm for plants to grow. Earth is like a gigantic greenhouse!

The Sun sends heat to Earth.

The Earth's atmosphere acts like a force field and bounces most of the heat back into space.

Atmosphere

GREENHOUSE EFFECT

Some of the heat stays on Earth, trapped by the atmosphere. The atmosphere is a layer of gases, including carbon dioxide and methane. These are called greenhouse gases.

We need some heat to stay on Earth because it keeps our planet warm enough to live on.

Can you spot five differences between these two pictures of a factory burning fossil fuel?

Carbon dioxide is the biggest bad gas! There is more of it in the air than any other greenhouse gas, and it's the main reason why Earth's temperatures are rising.

ENHANCED GREENHOUSE EFFECT

The enhanced greenhouse effect is caused when burning fossil fuels release a lot of greenhouse gases into the air. This makes the atmosphere thicker, so heat can't escape into space. This extra heat has led to global warming, and this causes climate change.

THEORY NO. 3 APPROVED

CLIMATE CHANGE

Ecologists study the changes that warmer temperatures force on the environment, plants, animals, and people. When any little thing changes in the environment, it has a knock-on effect.

ECO HERO ARCTIC MISSION REPORT

The Arctic is heating up two times faster than any other part of the world. Polar bears live, mate, and hunt there. So much ice has melted that the seals that polar bears eat have moved away.

This means polar bears don't have enough food and are dying. Polar bears are now considered an endangered species.

ACTIVITY

Write down when you've experienced extreme weather. What happened?

PRACTICAL NO. 4 APPROVED

○ **PETITION MINING COMPANIES**
Ask them to stop polluting the Arctic environment so polar bears have a better chance of surviving.

○ **POLAR BEARS AND PEOPLE DON'T MIX!**
Ask governments to send out patrols to keep bears away from towns, where they might be shot.

○ **COLLECT DATA ON POLAR BEAR POPULATIONS**
As soon as ecologists notice any problems, they can fly in and make suggestions to help the bears.

THE DAILY ECOLOGIST

CLIMATE CHANGE IS LEADING TO EXTREME WEATHER.

Which of these have you noticed happening where you live, or read about in the news?

FLOODING—the warmer temperatures pull lots of water into the air, causing huge rain storms.

RISING SEA LEVELS—melting ice is adding too much water to the oceans, and they are overflowing onto land.

DROUGHTS, HEAT WAVES, AND FIRES—higher temperatures make the dry parts of the world even drier and hotter.

HURRICANES AND TYPHOONS—warm water and warm air are the perfect ingredients for these dangerous storms.

TREE-RIFIC

Trees are superhero plants, but 15 billion are cut down every year. Eco Heroes, trees need your help!

When it rains, trees break up the flow of water, which helps stop flooding.

There are 3.1 trillion trees on Earth. There are more trees than stars in the Milky Way.

Trees are home to all kinds of birds, insects, and other animals—some are home to about 500 different species!

Trees make oxygen, which most living things need to survive.

Trees feed many animals, including millions of insects. One small apple tree can grow about 100 apples a year.

Tree roots suck up bad chemicals from soil and water. This helps stop water from carrying pollutants to the ocean.

Staring at trees can help us feel calm and happy.

One tree can gobble up about 50 lb. (22 kg) of carbon dioxide a year—the weight of a four-year-old!

Areas with lots of trees are known as a carbon sink because they suck lots of carbon dioxide out of the air. Trees use carbon dioxide to grow.

Trees provide shade to cool us off. This means we use less air-conditioning and make less pollution!

PRACTICAL 5

POLLUTION

We make pollution when we add harmful things to the environment. There are many types of pollution. Some pollution you can see, and some is invisible. But there are ways to reduce it!

WATER

Clean water keeps us, plants, and animals alive. When pollutants like trash, sewage, and oil end up in the water, they can kill the animals and plants living there.

NOISE

When loud noises go on for a long time, it can affect our sleep and scare animals. Noise pollution like boat engines confuses sea animals; it can cause whales to swim away.

ECO HERO ANTIPOLLUTION MISSION

◯ Don't buy single-use plastic, such as soda bottles.

◯ Don't put oil or chemicals down the sink.

◯ Walk, bike, or use public transportation.

◯ Turn lights off and reduce noise.

HOW FAR IS TOO FAR?

Air and water currents spread pollution all over the world. Plastic has even been found at Point Nemo, the farthest point from inhabited land.

LIGHT

Human-made light is turning nighttime into daytime. This changes the way nocturnal animals act: baby turtles follow bright lights onto roads when they should follow the moon out to sea.

AIR

You don't need X-ray vision to see smoke coming out of cars, factories, and chimneys. The smoke is a mixture of harmful gases and chemicals that pollutes our air and makes us sick.

PRACTICAL NO. 5 APPROVED

The first modern invention to use electricity was a single light bulb. Today we use so many billions of light bulbs, they can be seen from space.

LAND

Think of all the things you've thrown away today. A lot of it will end up in a landfill or even the ocean—where harmful chemicals leak out and hurt the environment.

ACTIVITY

How many pieces of trash are in the water?

BLUE PLANET

Earth is called the blue planet. Can you guess why? Water is the right answer! 71% of Earth's surface is covered by it.

THEORY NO. 5 APPROVED ★

Only about 2.5% of Earth's water is fresh and drinkable, which makes it very precious. And less than 1% of that water is found in places like rivers and lakes, where it is accessible. The rest of Earth's fresh water is stored in glaciers and rocks deep underground.

Two-thirds of our body is water. We can live for about 21 days without food but only about four without water.

FOOD FOR THOUGHT

70% of all fresh water is used to make food. Some foods use up more water than others:

It takes 450 gal. (1,700 L) of water to make 3.5 oz. (100 g) of chocolate. That's ten bathtubs of water!

If we cut back on how much we eat of these foods that use up a lot of water, that would help the environment.

It takes 1,860 gal. (7,040 L) of water to make 1 lb. (0.45 kg) of beef. That's 86 bathtubs of water!

Everything on Earth depends on clean water to survive, but these villains are poisoning it:

Poisonous chemical waste from factories, farms, and medicines is dumped into water and can harm people, plants, and animals.

Human sewage in some places flows straight into water and makes people and animals ill.

Global warming is causing droughts, and some countries run out of fresh water. They have to ship it in from other countries, which is expensive and pollutes the environment.

Ecologists are experimenting with smart ways to collect fresh water:

Fog collection: in very foggy areas, scientists put up mesh panels that collect mist. The mist turns into droplets, which are stored in a tank.

Desalination plants: these are factories where special machines take the salt out of sea water.

ECO HERO MISSION— TURN OFF THE FAUCET

Using less water can help everyone in the world. Here are some ideas on how to use less water:

- ◯ Plug the sink when you wash dishes.
- ◯ Take a shower instead of a bath.
- ◯ Wash fruits and vegetables in a bowl.
- ◯ Turn off annoying dripping faucets!

ACTIVITY

Can you think of any more ways to save water?

OCEANTASTIC

The ocean holds about 97% of the world's water. More than 50% of the world's plants and animals live in the ocean—and new ones are being found there all the time.

All over the world there are islands of trash floating in the ocean. The largest is called the Great Pacific Garbage Patch. There are 1.8 trillion pieces of plastic in this patch, and it weighs more than 500 jumbo jets.

Microalgae—microscopic ocean plants—gobble up about 2.5 billion tons of carbon dioxide a year—which helps slow down climate change. They also make 50% of the oxygen we breathe.

THEORY NO. 6 APPROVED ★

All the carbon dioxide in the ocean has made the water more acidic, and it kills sea animals like coral.

WHAT CAN ECOLOGISTS DO?

○ Come up with smart ideas to clean up the plastic.

○ Ask governments to form marine parks that protect everything inside them.

○ Study microorganisms such as algae to understand how they help the ocean.

○ Teach people how to fish more carefully.

The ocean soaks up heat from the Sun and then moves it around the world, helping keep the planet warm in the winter and cool in the summer. This is known as the Great Ocean Conveyor Belt.

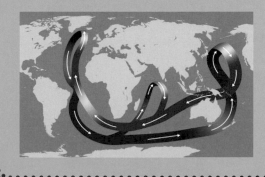

Old fishing nets make up a lot of the plastic in the ocean. Turtles, dolphins, and seals often get trapped in them and drown...

Turtles often eat plastic bags because they look like their favorite food— jellyfish.

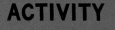

ACTIVITY

"Take 3 for the sea"—an Australian nonprofit suggests we pick up 3 pieces of trash wherever we are, to stop it from ending up in the ocean.

SUSTAINABILITY

Earth has many precious resources, such as water, air, oil, minerals, plants, and animals—but we have been using them up too quickly. The way we use them damages the planet, too.

One way to determine if you're living sustainably is to track your ecological footprint. Our footprint is how many resources are used to make all the things that we use—this can be food, water, our homes, the things we buy, and the ways we travel. The more sustainably we live, the smaller our footprint.

Ecological Footprint

✦ ECO HERO SUSTAINABILITY MISSION STATEMENT

Protect Earth's resources so people all around the world, future generations, and other living things have enough to survive. We can do this by living sustainably.

ECO HERO FASHION MISSION REPORT

A T-shirt's journey into your closet uses up a lot of resources.

Pesticides are used on cotton plants, which pollute the environment.

Some factories use poisonous chemicals that pollute the air and water.

Making a cotton T-shirt uses about 700 gal. (2,700 L) of water.

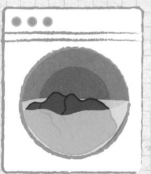

Washing and drying the T-shirt uses a lot of water and energy.

Shirts can be wrapped in nonrecyclable packaging.

Items are transported around the world on vehicles that produce greenhouse gases.

ECO SOLUTIONS

In organic farming, only natural pesticides are used. They don't hurt animals, plants, birds, insects, the land, or people!

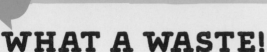

WHAT A WASTE!

Waste is everything we throw away. Often we get rid of things that are perfectly fine, like a T-shirt we no longer want. What we throw away and how we throw it away affects the environment. What happens to our waste?

1.4 billion tons of food gets thrown away every year—that's a third of everything that's made for us to eat.

RECYCLING:

This is when trash such as glass, plastic, and paper is turned into other things. What can be recycled depends on where you live, so check before adding items to your recycling bin.

COMPOST

This is food and yard waste. It can be collected and used to help plants grow in local parks.

SHIP IT

Some countries are running out of space for their waste, so they pay to ship it to other countries —which creates more pollution.

If you put something in the recycling bin that's not supposed to be there, it could ALL be thrown into the landfill. Always clean containers before you recycle them.

LANDFILL

Most waste is dumped in an enormous hole. It can take hundreds and hundreds of years for this waste to break down, and it gives off gases and chemicals that pollute land, water, and air.

INCINERATION PLANT

This is when waste is taken to a factory to be burned. The heat can be used to make electricity, but burning waste pollutes the air.

ACTIVITY

Which items should go in the COMPOST BOX and which in the RECYCLING?

PRACTICAL
NO. 6
APPROVED

WHAT TO DO ABOUT WASTE

REDUCE

If all the waste humans make in a year were loaded onto trucks, they would stretch around the world 24 times. Here are some of the things Eco Heroes can do to help.

99% of the things we buy are thrown out within 6 months.

One million plastic bottles are bought every minute. Most of them end up in landfills or in the ocean. Scientists think there could be more plastic than fish in the ocean by 2050.

Electronic items are the fastest-growing waste in the world. Companies don't make tablets and phones to last, so they are thrown away when we upgrade.

How long it takes some things to break down:

Aluminum can—100 years
Plastic bottle—500 years
Cell phone—NEVER

○ Buy fewer things. Think, "Do I need this?" before you buy something.

○ Borrow or swap things with your family or friends.

○ Say no to single-use items such as plastic bags, plastic bottles, and plastic silverware.

ZERO WASTE
Some people are so good at reducing that the waste they make in a year can fit inside a jar! This is called zero waste because it's such a tiny amount.

REUSE

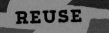

○ Find smart ways to reuse things before you throw them away. For example, keep glass jars for storing leftovers instead of using foil or plastic wrap, which are used once.

○ Turn old clothes into something new—jeans make good shorts, and T-shirts can become dishcloths.

○ If something is broken, can you fix it instead of throwing it?

RECYCLE

○ Not everything can be recycled. Paper, some plastic, glass, and metals are the most recycled materials. It's important to recycle because it means we use fewer natural resources.

○ If you see this symbol on something, then it can be recycled.

✏ ACTIVITY

Make a list of 5 things you can do to make a difference every day.

EXTINCTION EMERGENCY

We need to act now to help Earth's animals. Scientists think that 50% of all animal species are going to be gone forever by 2060 if we don't take Eco Hero steps to save them now.

Humans have taken over three-fourths of the planet's land. This does leave much space for animals to live, and it takes away their food.

THEORY
NO. 8
APPROVED

The pollution we put in the environment makes it hard for animals to live. Many species, including killer whales, are in danger of extinction because of poisonous chemicals in the ocean.

Ecologists spend a lot of time studying what animals need in order to help save them. Here are some super ideas that are currently in place around the world:

Hunting is a very big threat to animals. Some people hunt animals for fun, or for their fur or feathers. Others kill animals like elephants because they want to use their tusks for medicine or turn them into decorations like jewelry.

GIANT PANDA REPORT

Wild giant pandas have started to make a comeback in China. Almost 300 have been born in the past 15 years. Ecologists worked with the government to set up reserves and to reforest areas where pandas live, making sure plenty of bamboo was grown for pandas to eat. China also banned the hunting of giant pandas.

ACTIVITY

How many pandas can you find?

We have taken animals to countries where they don't belong. Once there, they often kill local wildlife by eating them or passing on diseases.

CAPTIVE BREEDING: this is when animals in places like zoos are brought together to mate and hopefully have babies.

REINTRODUCTION: this is when animals born in captivity are put back into the wild.

WILDLIFE CORRIDORS: protected areas of land let animals travel from one habitat to another to reach the natural resources that they need to live.

BUG LOVE

Insects might be small, but they have a huge part to play in life on Earth.

Scientists think there are 10 quintillion (10,000,000,000,000,000,000) insects on our planet! That's more than 200 million insects for each human on the planet. That might sound like a lot of insects, but there used to be many, many more.

More than 40% of insect families are in danger of dying out. Insects are vital to our existence!

POLLINATION

Insects carry pollen between plants, helping new ones grow. These plants give us vegetables, fruits, and nuts to eat. The crops that honeybees pollinate feed almost 90% of the world. That means one out of every three bites of food we eat is made by bees.

FOOD

Many people and animals eat insects. Some, like crickets and ants, are very good for us—they're full of protein, vitamins, and minerals. Others make food that we like to eat, such as honey. We also use honey as a medicine.

HOW CAN WE HELP?

Some of the chemicals that farmers and gardeners use to make plants grow faster can poison the soil and kill insects—not just the pests. One thing we can do is to buy organic foods that don't use these chemicals. Or even better, grow your own!

PESTS

Some insects, like flies, spread diseases. Nature has its own way to control them. Look around—can you spot a spiderweb with a dead fly in it? That's dinner for the spider!

ACTIVITY

Which creature in the garden doesn't belong?

GARDENERS

Insects help plants grow naturally. When insects move around, they make tunnels to carry water to plants, and their poop adds healthy nutrients.

MIGHTY MICROBES

Dust off your lab coat, Eco Hero! It's time to take a look at tiny living creatures that can only be seen with a microscope—microbes! Plankton, fungi, bacteria, and microalgae are examples of microbes.

MICROBES are all around us—in the air, land, and water—and they're also inside us, helping us stay healthy.

THEORY NO. 10 APPROVED

Microbes will eat almost anything! Scientists have discovered a bacterium that can eat plastic, and they hope to use it in the global fight against plastic pollution.

PLANKTON are microbes found in the ocean and are the main food source for a lot of sea life. These tiny microbes will eat pollution and turn it into something less harmful! Unfortunately, plankton can be killed by human-made pollution. When plankton die, the creatures that eat them—and the animals that eat those creatures—die, too.

FUNGI are things like mold and mushrooms. There are types of fungi that gobble up oil spills, sewage, and even nuclear waste!

MICROALGAE are plantlike organisms that are food for ocean animals.

BACTERIA help make some food, such as cheese. Many antibiotics are made from bacteria.

CITIZEN SCIENCE

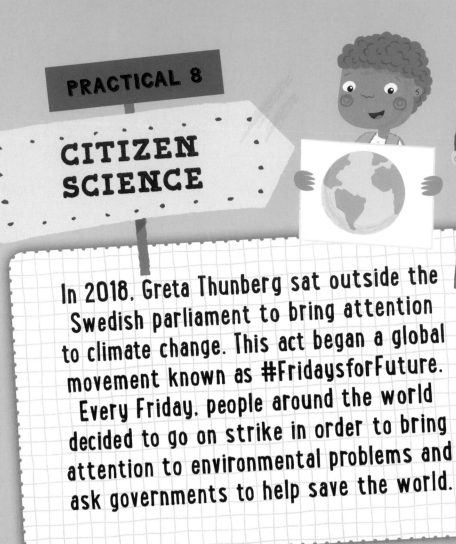

In 2018, Greta Thunberg sat outside the Swedish parliament to bring attention to climate change. This act began a global movement known as #FridaysforFuture. Every Friday, people around the world decided to go on strike in order to bring attention to environmental problems and ask governments to help save the world.

 ECO HERO CITIZEN SCIENTISTS

Volunteer citizen scientists around the world collect data on living things, and a lot of it helps the environment. It's free, and some projects can even be done in your pajamas! Projects include:

O Spending an hour writing down all the birds that fly past your window. Ecologists will use data like this to see a bird's migration journey.

O Recording the pollution on your local beach. If there's a lot, ecologists will arrange a cleanup project to remove the litter.

DATES FOR YOUR ECO HERO CALENDAR:

JAN	FEB	MAR	APR
		World Wildlife Day—March 3	Earth Day —usually April 22
MAY	**JUN**	**JUL**	**AUG**
	World Environment Day—June 5 World Oceans Day—June 8		
SEP	**OCT**	**NOV**	**DEC**
Clean Up the World Campaign—third weekend of September		Buy Nothing Day— late November	

RACHEL CARSON

Rachel Carson was the first person to show that pesticides harm the environment. Thanks to Rachel, people started to take more of an interest in fixing environmental problems.

GEORGE WASHINGTON CARVER

George Washington Carver invented many ways to keep soil healthy for growing crops. He advised world leaders like Mahatma Gandhi on agriculture and nutrition.

CHARLES DARWIN

Charles Darwin was the first scientist to explain that living things like animals and birds can change over time in order to fit into the environment they live in.

HALL

JANE GOODALL

This ecologist's work shows us that people are part of the animal kingdom. She has spent almost 60 years in the wild, closely watching chimpanzees to understand them better.

WANGARI MAATHAI

Wangari Maathai started a movement to replant trees in Kenya, which successfully helped make the environment better. In 2004 she received the Nobel Peace Prize for her work.

OF FAME

NAOMI KLEIN

An author and conservationist, Naomi Klein is a very important voice in the fight against climate change. Her campaigning has made some governments agree to phase out fossil fuels.

DAVID ATTENBOROUGH

A naturalist, TV host, and conservationist, David Attenborough has written some of the world's most important TV shows about Earth. About 20 different plants and animals have been named after him!

GRETA THUNBERG

In August 2018, Greta Thunberg sat down outside Sweden's parliament to strike for the climate. She started a worldwide movement, and millions have joined her.

EXAMINATION

Now it's time to see how much you have learned.

1 Where can you find pollution?
   a) Land
   b) Water
   c) Air
   d) All of the above

2 What is a natural resource?
   a) Material produced by Earth
   b) Something that falls out of the sky
   c) Something you find in a toy store

3 What is the biosphere?
   a) A very big ball
   b) Planet Earth
   c) A desert

4 What is coral?
   a) A skeleton
   b) A tiny animal
   c) A stone

5 What are fossil fuels made from?
   a) Really old cars
   b) Trash
   c) Dead plants and animals

6 Which of these is a greenhouse gas?
   a) Oxygen
   b) Carbon dioxide
   c) Pesticide

7 Where do polar bears live?
   a) In the Caribbean
   b) In the Arctic
   c) In Antarctica

8 Which gas do trees use to grow?
   a) Carbon dioxide
   b) Oxygen
   c) Methane

9 What was the first modern invention to use electricity?

   a) A car

   b) A microwave

   c) A light bulb

10 How much of Earth is covered in water?

   a) 99%

   b) 50%

   c) 71%

11 What is the largest island of trash called?

   a) Great Pacific Garbage Island

   b) Great Pacific Garbage Patch

   c) Great Pacific Garbage Land

12 What happens to trash at an incineration plant?

   a) It's recycled

   b) It's burned

   c) It's composted

13 How long does it take for a cell phone to break down?

   a) It never will

   b) 500 years

   c) 6 years

14 Where are giant pandas found?

   a) United States

   b) China

   c) Africa

ECO SCORES

Check your answers at the back of the book and add up your score.

1 to 5 Oops! Go back and brush up on your eco facts.

6 to 10 You are well on your way to becoming a top ecologist.

11 to 14 Top of the class! You really know your stuff!

ECO SPEAK

Climate
The long-term weather and temperature in a particular area of the world.

Data
Information, sometimes made of numbers, that we use to learn about something.

Endangered
An animal or plant that has very low numbers and might become extinct.

Environment
All the things around us, including nature and wildlife.

Extinct
Animals or plants that are no longer alive.

Global
Having to do with the whole Earth.

Microbe
A living thing that can only be seen under a microscope.

Oxygen
A colorless gas. Most living things need it to survive.

Pesticide
Poisonous chemicals made to kill certain types of insects.

Research
Careful study of something to learn about it.

Sanctuary
Land or water where animals are protected.

Species
Animals or plants that can reproduce.

ECO ACADEMY

GOOD JOB!

You made it through your eco training.

Name...

FULLY QUALIFIED

ECO HERO

Page 7
Water and a banana are natural resources

Page 9
You would not pack a trumpet

Page 13

Page 17

Page 22-23
There are seven pieces of trash

Page 31
The apples and banana belong in the compost box. The newspaper, plastic bottle, and can belong in the recycling bin

Page 35
There are five pandas:

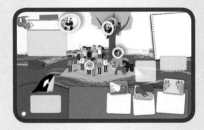

Page 36-37
The octopus doesn't belong

Pages 48
1=d, 2=a, 3=b, 4=b, 5=c, 6=b, 7=a, 8=a, 9=c, 10= c, 11=b, 12=b, 13=a, 14=b